DK SUPER Planet

Place and Time

MAPPING OUR WORLD

Discover how maps are essential to finding our way around the world

Produced for DK by
Editorial Just Content Limited
Design Studio Noel

Author Steve Tomecek

Senior Editor Amelia Jones
Senior Art Editor Gilda Pacitti
Managing Editor Katherine Neep
Managing Art Editor Sarah Corcoran
Production Editor Jaypal Chauhan
Production Controller Rebecca Parton
Publisher Sarah Forbes
Managing Director, Learning Hilary Fine

First American Edition, 2025
Published in the United States by DK Publishing,
a division of Penguin Random House LLC
1745 Broadway, 20th Floor, New York, NY 10019

Copyright © 2025 Dorling Kindersley Limited
25 26 27 28 29 10 9 8 7 6 5 4 3 2 1
001–345412–Mar/2025

All rights reserved.
Without limiting the rights under the copyright reserved
above, no part of this publication may be reproduced, stored
in or introduced into a retrieval system, or transmitted, in any
form, or by any means (electronic, mechanical, photocopying,
recording, or otherwise), without the prior written permission
of the copyright owner.
Published in Great Britain by Dorling Kindersley Limited

A catalog record for this book
is available from the Library of Congress.
HC ISBN: 978-0-5939-6262-6
PB ISBN: 978-0-5939-6261-9

DK books are available at special discounts when purchased
in bulk for sales promotions, premiums, fund-raising,
or educational use.
For details, contact: DK Publishing Special Markets,
1745 Broadway, 20th Floor, New York, NY 10019
SpecialSales@dk.com

Printed and bound in China

www.dk.com

Contents

What Are Maps?	4
Why Do We Need Maps?	6
Map Keys and Symbols	8
Map Scales	10
The Globe	12
Compass Directions	14
Latitude and Longitude	16
Longitude and Time Zones	18
Hemispheres	20
Topographic and Physical Maps	22
Historical Maps	24
Thematic Maps	26
Mapping Climate Change	28
Transit Maps	30
Modern Mapping	32
Everyday Science: Navigating by the Stars	34
Everyday Science: Geocaching	36
Let's Experiment: Make a Treasure Map	38
Let's Experiment: Make a Compass	40
Vocabulary Builder: A Hike to Remember	42
Glossary	44
Index	46

What Are MAPS?

For thousands of years, **maps** have been helping people find their way. A map is a model that shows where things are located in relation to each other. Most maps are flat drawings. This makes it difficult to show round or bumpy things, like Earth. But mapmakers have figured out a way.

Treasure maps show the location of buried treasure. They use **landmarks** like trees and rivers to help treasure seekers find it.

Physical maps use different colors to show what the land looks like, including mountains, forests, and bodies of water.

Political maps show **boundaries**, like **continents**, countries, and cities. Political maps change when boundaries are redrawn.

Floor plans are maps that show the different rooms in a building. They can help you find your way around a building.

City maps are very useful. They show the names of roads. They also show the locations of parks and landmarks.

Fascinating fact

One of the oldest maps in the world comes from what is now Türkiye. It is over 8,000 years old.

Why Do We Need MAPS?

Geography is the study of land, people, and the environment around us. One of the most important tools geographers use is maps. Geographers are scientists who use maps to understand the world and its natural features. They also use maps to compare things like **climate**, **population**, and natural resources in different places around the world.

Maps can also show patterns. This map of the Ring of Fire shows earthquake activity in the Pacific Ocean.

Fascinating fact

More than 1 billion people use **Google Maps** every month.

This map shows the four climate zones worldwide. The coldest areas are dark blue, while the hottest are red.

Maps help people find their way around without getting lost. This is important if you are traveling somewhere new.

Maps can show the **waterways** in a place, like this map of rivers in the USA.

Road maps show how to get from one place to another. They show main roads, smaller roads, and sometimes rest areas.

Trail maps can help you find your way when you are on a hike. They show paths, lakes, streams, hills, and swamps.

Street maps often include locations of famous buildings and other attractions. Some even show bus and train routes.

Map Keys and SYMBOLS

People who make maps are called **cartographers**. They use special drawings called map **symbols** to make maps easier to read. These symbols show important features and landmarks. Some show natural features such as rivers, lakes, and mountains. Others show special buildings, such as hospitals, schools, and libraries.

In the past, cartographers drew maps and symbols by hand, like the one shown in the picture above. It is over 400 years old.

Fascinating fact

Map symbols can be traced back over 25,000 years. People who lived in what is now Czechia carved them on a map on a mammoth tusk.

Today, most cartographers use computers to create maps and **keys**. It makes the process quicker and more accurate.

8

Maps with symbols have a special box called a key or **legend** that tells you what each symbol means.

Map **scale**

MAP KEY

- City park
- Central bank
- City hospital
- City hall
- River
- Science museum
- City library
- City high school

9

Map SCALES

Cartographers usually draw maps to scale. This means the **distances** between objects on a map are the same relative size as they are in real life. They are just much smaller. If you want to know the distance between objects on the map, you can use the map scale to calculate it.

On long hikes, people can use map scales to calculate how far they have to travel to get to their next stop.

USING MAP SCALES
Look at the map on the next page. Let's find out the distance between the library and the school.

1 Find the map scale. It looks like a small bar near the map key.

2 The distance marked on the scale tells you that 1 centimeter on this map is equal to 1.24 miles (2 km) in real life.

3 To find the distance between the school and library, use the map scale to measure the distance between the two places in centimeters.

4 Since the scale on this map is 1 cm = 2 km, multiply the distance you measured by 2. This is the actual distance you have to travel between the two places.

Find out!
Use a real map to find out the distance from your house to your school.

THE GLOBE

If you want to understand what Earth looks like, you can't beat a **globe**. Think of a globe as a scale model that shows what Earth looks like from space. Globes show the continents and oceans. And most show the world's countries. Geographers have been making and using globes for over 500 years.

Because Earth is shaped like a ball, it is impossible to accurately represent all its features on a flat map.

Fascinating fact

The largest rotating globe in the world is known as Eartha. It is located in Maine. Eartha is over 41.5 ft (12.6 m) in diameter.

Unlike globes, flat maps distort the size of land masses near the poles. Greenland is actually 14 times smaller than Africa.

Some globes show physical features on Earth's surface, such as lakes, rivers, mountain ranges, deserts, and even glaciers.

Maps and globes show many of the same features. But unlike flat maps, globes can accurately show the shapes of the continents.

Most globes have a stand. This allows them to spin and show Earth's tilt as it travels around the Sun.

13

Compass DIRECTIONS

Before maps, we used the Sun and stars to find our way around. In the **Northern Hemisphere**, the polestar became the direction north. Its opposite became south. Since the Sun rises and sets in a pattern, this gave us the directions east and west. All together, these are the **cardinal directions**.

On a map, a **compass** rose shows the cardinal directions. If you are facing north, then east is on your right.

Compasses can also tell you where north is. Magnetic compasses were first invented more than 2,000 years ago.

All modern maps have something called a compass rose or a north arrow. This helps you turn the map in the direction you would like to face.

To use a magnetic compass, hold it flat. Slowly turn until the needle points to the letter N. You are now facing north.

Fascinating fact

The word compass comes from Latin. It means "step together."

The needle points to Earth's magnetic pole. This is not the same as true north, which is at the very top of Earth.

Some people still use the Sun and the stars to help them find their way.

15

Latitude and **LONGITUDE**

Las Vegas

36°10′30″N
115°08′11″W

If you look at a world map, you will see a pattern of lines crossing each other. This grid is made of lines of **latitude** and **longitude**. These imaginary lines help people describe where different places on Earth are. They also help people locate or **navigate** to different places.

Coordinates are special numbers that help us find the exact location of a place on a map. They are written like this: latitude, longitude.

Since Earth is a sphere, latitude and longitude are measured in degrees. Degrees are also used to measure a circle.

Longitude is measured starting at the **prime meridian**. The prime meridian circles the center of Earth.

Latitude is measured starting at the **equator**. The equator circles the center of Earth.

Lines of longitude are vertical lines that circle Earth from north to south. They are farthest apart along the equator and come together at the poles.

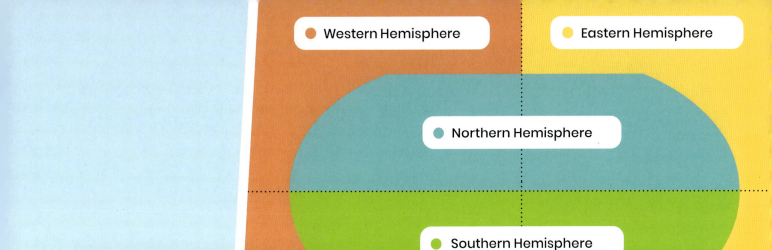

- Western Hemisphere
- Eastern Hemisphere
- Northern Hemisphere
- Southern Hemisphere

We use lines of latitude and longitude to divide Earth into four **hemispheres**.

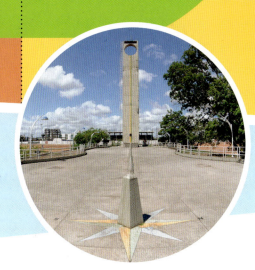

Lines of latitude are horizontal lines that circle Earth from east to west. They are parallel to each other, which means they never cross.

Equator

Macapá is a city in Brazil that sits right on the Equator. There's a place called the Marco Zero monument where you can stand with one foot in the Northern Hemisphere and the other in the Southern Hemisphere, at the same time. It's like being in two different parts of the Earth all at once!

Find out!

What is the latitude and longitude of the place where you live?

17

Longitude and
TIME ZONES

Earth is divided into **time zones.** Before the 19th century, these time zones did not exist. But as the world relied more on trains, the need for standardized time zones grew. In 1876, an engineer proposed dividing the world into 24 time zones.

As you move east from the prime meridian, you gain one hour for each time zone. As you move west, you lose one hour.

The prime meridian runs through Greenwich, in London, UK. It is set as the 0 hour.

The **international date line** runs opposite the prime meridian.

The US has six time zones.

If you keep changing time zones, you will eventually run out of hours in the day. This is why we have the international date line.

Mountain
Pacific
Eastern
Alaskan
Central
Hawaiian

When you cross west over the international date line, you jump ahead one day. If you cross east, you turn back one day. Tokyo, Japan, is almost a full day ahead of Honolulu, Hawai'i. If it is 8am on a Monday in Honolulu, that means it is 3am on Tuesday in Tokyo.

Fascinating fact

The international date line bends around several islands in the Pacific Ocean. This is so the islands are not split into two different days.

HEMISPHERES

The equator divides Earth into the Northern and Southern Hemispheres. Most of the land masses on Earth are found in the Northern Hemisphere. These include Europe, Asia, North America, about half of Africa, and a small piece of South America. The rest of South America, plus Australia and Antarctica, are in the Southern Hemisphere.

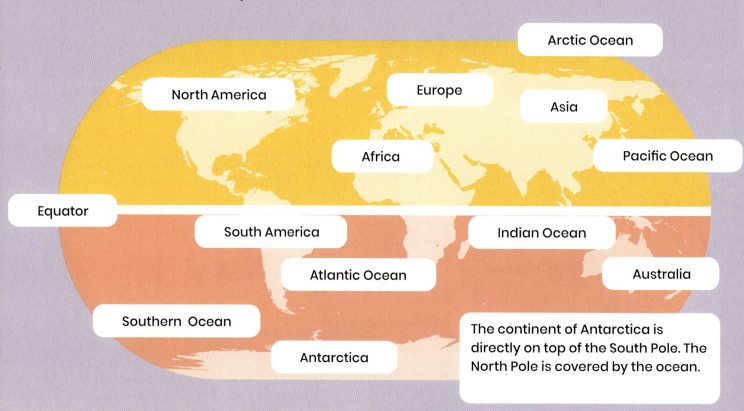

The continent of Antarctica is directly on top of the South Pole. The North Pole is covered by the ocean.

Fascinating fact

If you are in the Northern Hemisphere, the June **solstice** marks the start of summer. But if you are in the Southern Hemisphere, it is the December solstice that starts summer.

The poles affect how ocean water moves around Earth. This impacts climate and weather patterns on the continents.

It takes about one year for Earth to **orbit** the Sun. Because Earth's axis is tilted, it affects how sunlight hits Earth's surface.

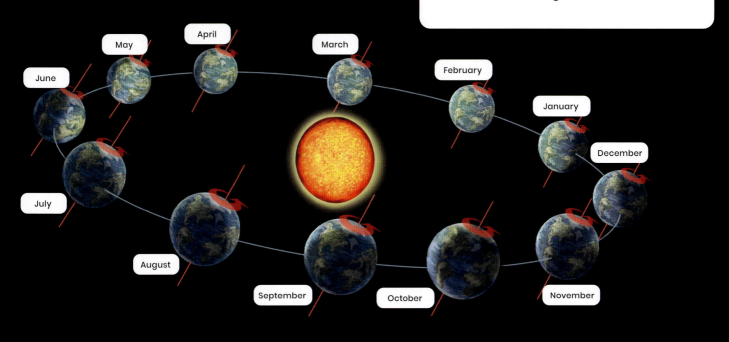

Earth's axis

Earth spins around an imaginary line called the **axis** of **rotation**. Earth's rotation is what gives us day and night.

The Northern and Southern Hemispheres get different amounts of sunlight at different times of the year. This gives us **seasons**.

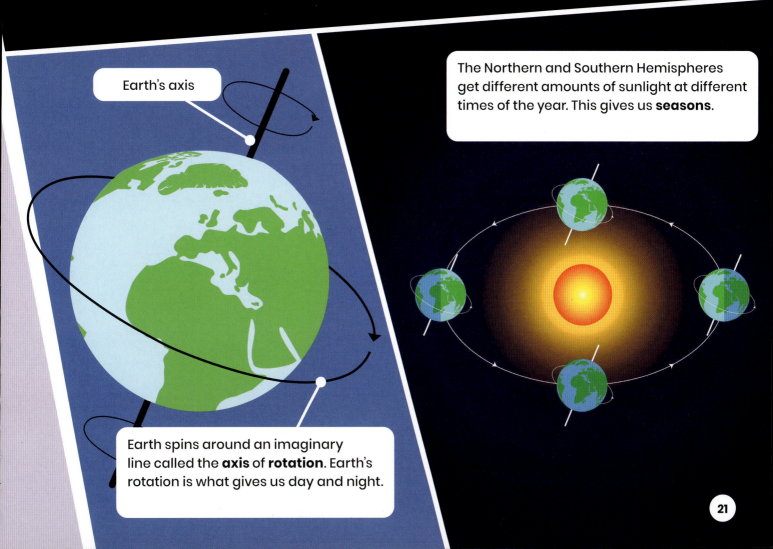

Topographic and PHYSICAL MAPS

To get a sense of what Earth's surface looks like, you need to use a physical map. Physical maps show major cities and towns, but their main purpose is to show landforms and bodies of water. Some show the **elevations** of mountains and the locations of other features, like forests and deserts.

Physical maps show information about Earth's surface. On the map below, you can see lakes, rivers, and mountain ranges of North America.

This three-dimensional physical map shows a part of Colorado. It helps show what the surface of the land looks like.

22

Topographic maps use special symbols called **contour lines**, which create a three-dimensional view of Earth's surface.

Contour lines are used to show areas of equal elevation.

Physical and topographic maps are not just used for land. **Bathymetric maps** show what Earth's surface looks like underwater. They indicate water depth.

Hikers, engineers, and scientists use topographic maps to understand what physical features are present in an area.

Find out!

Can you find a topographic map of your area? Check your local library or ask your teacher.

You need a topographic map to get the most detailed view of Earth's surface.

23

Historical
MAPS

Since people first started making them, maps have changed a lot. One big change is the material they are made with. Today, most maps are printed on paper. But long ago, maps were carved on materials like stones and clay tablets. These historical maps can give us clues about the people who made them.

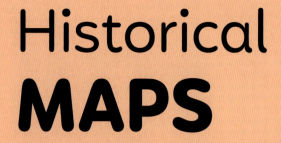

The *Theatrum Orbis Terrarum* is considered the first atlas, or book of maps. It was printed in 1570 **CE**.

Fascinating fact

The oldest known map is the sky map discovered in Lascaux, a network of caves in France. The map dates back around 17,000 years and shows three stars.

The Imago Mundi map was carved into clay around the 6th century **BCE**. It shows Babylon, surrounding areas, and bodies of water.

This Anglo-Saxon world map was made between 1025 and 1050 CE. It is probably based on a Roman map.

The Turin Papyrus Map dates to around 1150 BCE. It shows where stone quarries were located in Ancient Egypt.

The Bedolina Map was carved into rock between 1000 and 200 BCE. It is one of the oldest topographic maps, and shows fields and villages.

25

Thematic MAPS

Information about what is happening in different places around the world can be presented in maps. This allows people to compare them and see changes over time. Maps that show specific information are called thematic maps. They can show things that relate to an area's climate, **economy**, or population.

Thematic maps can show lots of information about people, including their age, their education, and how much money they have. They can make complicated information simpler to understand.

Thematic maps are not just about people. They are about places, too. This map shows how much water is available around the world. The lighter blue areas have less water, and the darker blue ares have more.

In order to collect accurate data for thematic maps, measurements need to be taken around the world.

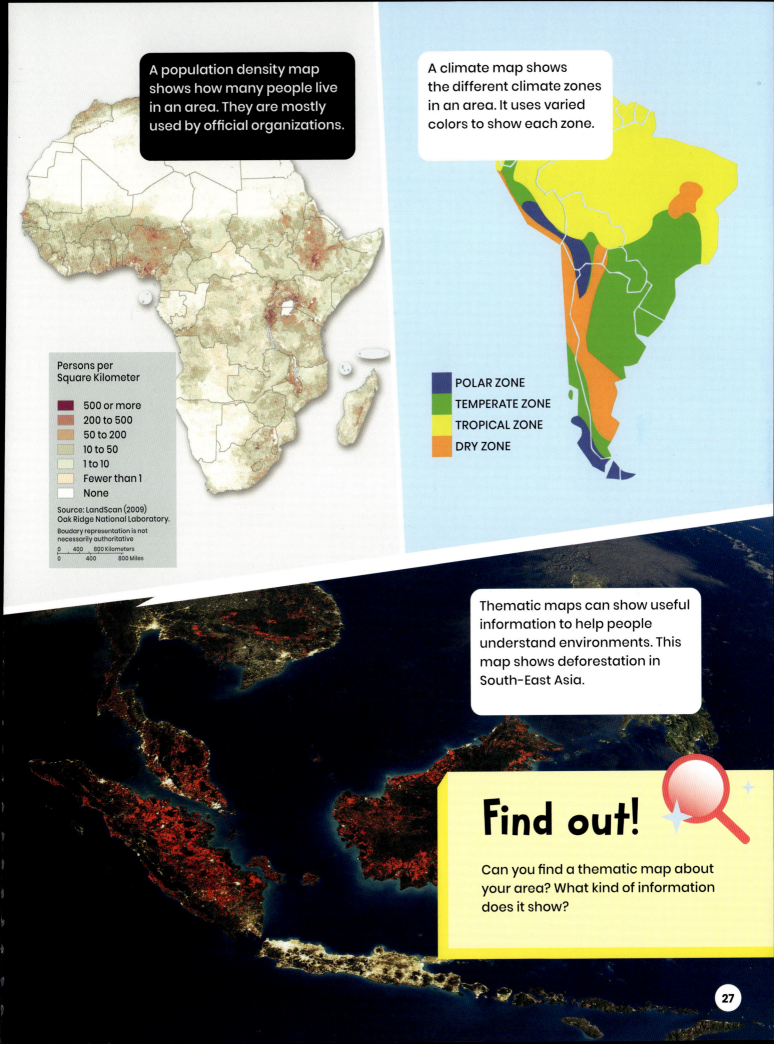

A population density map shows how many people live in an area. They are mostly used by official organizations.

A climate map shows the different climate zones in an area. It uses varied colors to show each zone.

Persons per Square Kilometer
- 500 or more
- 200 to 500
- 50 to 200
- 10 to 50
- 1 to 10
- Fewer than 1
- None

Source: LandScan (2009) Oak Ridge National Laboratory.
Boudary representation is not necessarily authoritative

0 400 800 Kilometers
0 400 800 Miles

- POLAR ZONE
- TEMPERATE ZONE
- TROPICAL ZONE
- DRY ZONE

Thematic maps can show useful information to help people understand environments. This map shows deforestation in South-East Asia.

Find out!

Can you find a thematic map about your area? What kind of information does it show?

Mapping
CLIMATE CHANGE

Scientists can use maps to track the impact of climate change. Maps can help scientists monitor climate data, like temperatures. They can also compare conditions in the past to the present. This lets scientists see where problems are and how fast changes are happening.

Scientists use maps to make predictions. They come up with solutions to help reduce climate change's impact in the future.

1980

2012

Scientists use satellites to make detailed maps of Earth. These two maps show that Arctic ice has shrunk dramatically between 1980 and 2012.

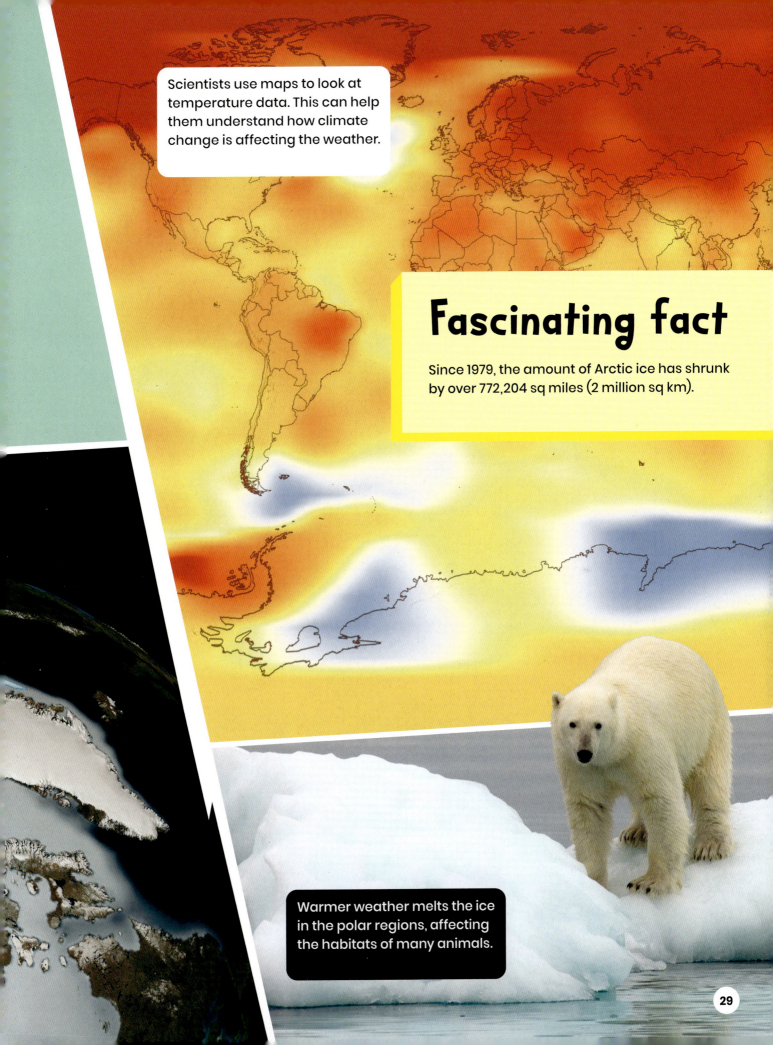

Scientists use maps to look at temperature data. This can help them understand how climate change is affecting the weather.

Fascinating fact

Since 1979, the amount of Arctic ice has shrunk by over 772,204 sq miles (2 million sq km).

Warmer weather melts the ice in the polar regions, affecting the habitats of many animals.

Transit MAPS

Imagine you have arrived in a new city. You want to use public transportation to get around. The best way to figure out which bus or train to take is to use a transit map. These maps show different routes in different colors. They include stops and transfer points. Some show major attractions, like museums, schools, libraries, and government buildings.

More than 3 million people ride the New York City subway each day.

Subway maps use something called schematization. It means that the lines on the map are straightened out, and the stations are spaced evenly so that they're easy to find.

30

Fascinating fact

The London Underground map was first developed in 1931. It is one of the most famous transit maps in the world. It is known for its clear and easy-to-read design.

Train maps often look like this. They show stations and use color-coding so it is easy to see which lines go where.

Bus maps often show timetables, ticket prices, and routes.

The London Underground travels a total length of around 250 miles (402 km) across its network.

Modern MAPPING

For centuries, maps have been printed on paper. Now more people are using digital maps. Digital maps have many advantages over printed maps. They can be updated almost instantly. And they can put the world in the palm of your hand. They are also scalable. You can zoom out to a country or zoom in to street level.

Thanks to the Global Positioning System (GPS), your phone can show your exact location when you open a map app.

Most smartphones come with map apps. These show you where you are and plot the best route to a destination.

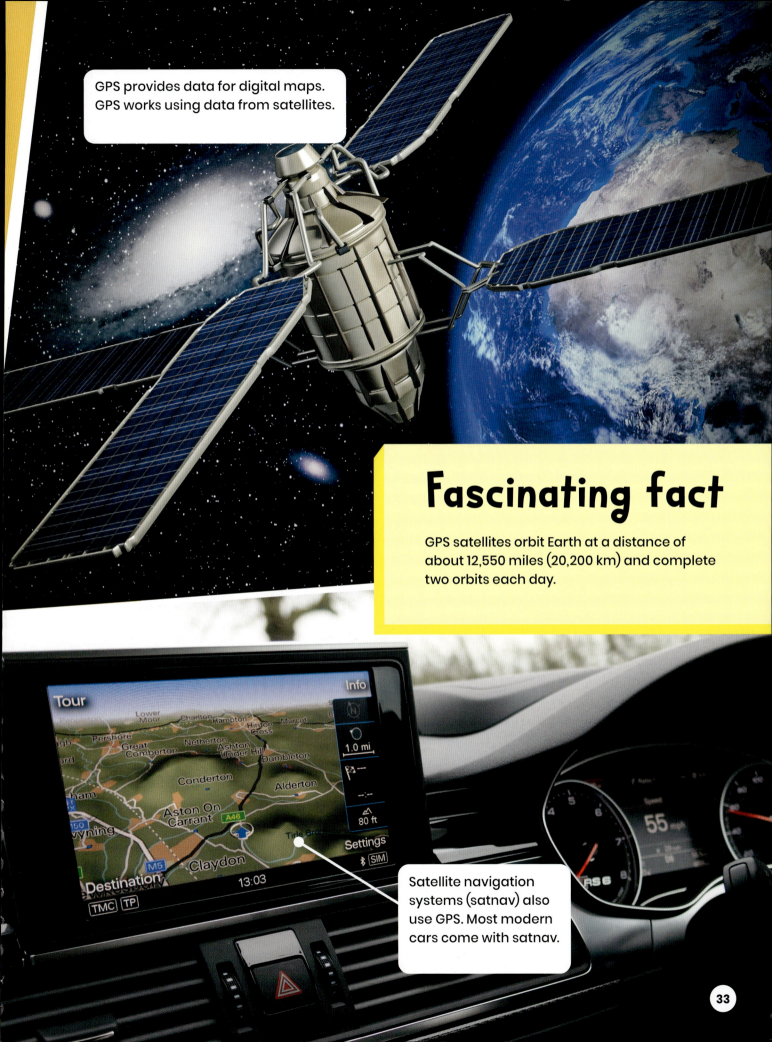

GPS provides data for digital maps. GPS works using data from satellites.

Fascinating fact

GPS satellites orbit Earth at a distance of about 12,550 miles (20,200 km) and complete two orbits each day.

Satellite navigation systems (satnav) also use GPS. Most modern cars come with satnav.

Everyday SCIENCE
Navigating by the Stars

Before we had compasses and GPS, we navigated using the stars. If you live in the Northern Hemisphere, you can use **Polaris**, or the North Star, to get around at night. Polaris is not as bright as you might think. As Earth rotates, other stars seem to move. But Polaris stays in the same place.

Polaris is directly over the North Pole, which is why it does not appear to move at night.

Sailors use a piece of equipment called a sextant to see the angle of Polaris in the sky. It tells them how far north they are.

Everyday SCIENCE
Geocaching

Do you enjoy scavenger hunts? Then you might like **geocaching**. It follows the same idea, but uses GPS and online clues. The goal is to find something (the "cache") that another game player has stashed in an out-of-the-way place. There are over 3 million geocaches hidden around the world.

1 First, someone hides the cache. The cache is a small box where the person places some "treasure" to be found, such as a small toy. The cache also contains a logbook.

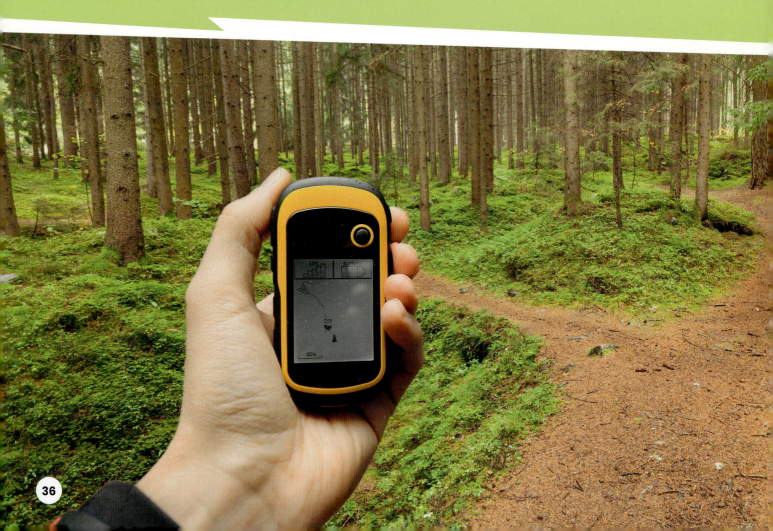

2 The cache is hidden where it will not easily be seen, like in a hollow log, between rocks, or under a bench.

3 Next, the person who hid the cache posts clues online so players can find it. The clues include precise longitude and latitude readings.

4 The player searches for the cache using GPS. But they can only get within 30 ft (9 m) of it using GPS. Then, they have to use their senses to find it.

5 When they find the cache, the player opens the box and signs the logbook. This shows they were there.

6 The player can take the treasure out of the geocache. But if they do, they must put something else in.

37

Let's EXPERIMENT!

MAKE A TREASURE MAP

Become a creative cartographer by making your own treasure map! You can make it look more realistic by staining and crumpling the paper, so it looks like it has been passed down through the ages.

You will need:
- Paper
- Cold tea or coffee
- A blow-dryer
- A pen

1 Take a piece of paper. Crumple it up into a ball. Uncrumple the paper. Lay it flat on a table or other surface.

2 Sprinkle some cold tea or coffee on the paper. The color will help it look old.

3 Dry the paper with a blow-dryer set to a low setting.

4 Use the pen to draw your map. Don't forget to add an X to mark the treasure!

A MAP FROM 1582

Maps have changed a lot over the years. This map was made in Spain in 1582. It shows South America. But really, it shows what the people who made it thought South America looked like. You might recognize some names on it, like Peru and Brazil.

39

Let's EXPERIMENT!

MAKE A COMPASS

People have used compasses for hundreds of years to help them find their way. In this experiment, you will make your own.

You will need:
- A needle
- A magnet
- Adhesive putty
- A cork
- A bowl of water

1 Carefully hold a needle by the eye (the hole at the blunt end).

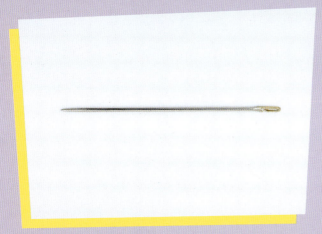

2 Rub the needle on the magnet 50 times. Make sure you lift the needle off the magnet each time.

3 Put some adhesive putty on top of a cork. Then put the needle on top of the putty.

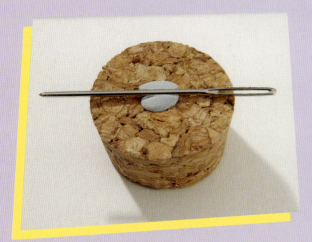

4 Get a bowl of water. Put the cork in the water. It will move until the eye of the needle is pointing north.

COMPASS CONFUSION AT THE POLES

Explorers at the North and South Poles have a tough time using compasses. Normally, a compass needle points north, but near the poles, it gets confused and may point up or down instead. Because of this, explorers use tools like GPS. They also look at the Sun and stars for direction.

Vocabulary BUILDER
A Hike to Remember

People use maps to navigate the great outdoors. Read the journal entry to find out how one hiker and her father ascended and descended a high mountain. Pay attention to key words that describe how the map and other tools helped them understand and plan for the terrain they would be climbing.

> After driving to the **trailhead**, Dad took out the topographic map. The mountain's elevation is 3,554 ft (1,083 m), so we knew it would be a long day.
>
> There are two trails to the **summit**. We measured them with the map scale and ruler. The blue trail was about 3 miles (4.8 km) but the contour lines were close together at the top—a steep climb! The red trail was about 5 miles (8 km) long but looked easier.
>
> We took the red trail up and the blue trail down. Dad handed me the compass and said I was our guide. Using the trail map and key, I kept us on track. When we reached the summit, the view was amazing! Dad used his pocket GPS to check our exact longitude and latitude, which matched the **survey marker** at the top.

Tools for a hike	compass, contour line, GPS, latitude, longitude, map key, map scale, ruler, topographic map, trail map
Parts of a hike	ascent, climb, descent, elevation, path, summit, survey marker, top, trailhead, view
Descriptive words	close, easy, far, fast, gradual, hard, long, slow, steep, tiring

Imagine you are hiking up a hill or mountain near you.

How would you use a map to get to the top?

Use the words in the vocabulary box above, and the example on page 42 to describe your hike.

Glossary

Axis A line that runs through the center of a spinning object, dividing it into two halves.

Bathymetric map A map that shows the depth and shape of underwater surfaces.

BCE Before Common Era.

Boundary Something that marks the edge or limit.

Cardinal directions The main points of a compass—north, south, east, and west.

Cartographer A person who makes maps.

CE Common Era. It is a way to count the years in the calendar we use today.

Compass A tool for finding direction.

Continent Any one of the seven great landmasses on Earth.

Contour lines Lines that show how steep or flat land is.

Distance A measure between things, such as objects.

Economy The system of making, using, and trading goods in an area, such as a town or country.

Elevation The height of a landform, such as a mountain, from sea level.

Equator An imaginary line that runs east to west around the center of Earth, measured at 0° latitude.

Geocaching A GPS-based game where players find items hidden at geographic coordinates.

Geography The study of Earth's natural features and atmosphere, and how they affect people and the environment.

Globe A three-dimensional map of Earth.

Google Maps A web service that gives detailed geographic information.

Hemisphere One of the halves that Earth is divided into—either the west and east, or the north and south.

International date line A line that runs at roughly the anti-meridian, or 180° longitude, and acts as a boundary between one day and the next.

Key A feature on a map that describes or explains what the different map symbols mean, also called a legend.

Landmark Describes a point in a landscape that is used as a reference or marks a boundary.

Latitude Imaginary lines that run east to west and measure distances on Earth.

Legend A feature on a map that describes or explains what the different map symbols mean, also called a key.

Longitude Imaginary lines that run north to south and measure distances on Earth.

Map A two-dimensional model of Earth that shows where different things are in relation to each other.

Navigate To find or plan your way somewhere or through something.

Northern Hemisphere The top half of Earth, from the equator to the North Pole.

Orbit A path that one space object, such as a planet, regularly takes around another one, such as a star.

Physical map A map that shows the physical features of Earth's surface, namely landforms and bodies of water.

Polaris The star toward which the northern end of the Earth's axis nearly points (also known as the North Star).

Population The total number of people in an area, such as a city or region.

Prime meridian The imaginary line that divides Earth into two equal parts (Eastern Hemisphere and Western Hemisphere), used as the basis for world time zones.

Rotation The act of moving in a circle.

Scale A measure of the relative distances on a map used to calculate actual distances.

Season One of the periods in the year characterized by different weather.

Southern Hemisphere The bottom half of Earth, from the equator to the South Pole.

Summit The top of a hill or mountain.

Survey marker A small sign or object placed on the ground to show where measurements are taken.

Symbol Something, such as an illustration, that represents something else.

Time zone An area consisting of 15° longitude where a standard time is used.

Topographic map A physical map that uses contour lines to show elevations of landforms and water depths.

Trailhead Where a trail begins.

Waterway A long body of water that boats can travel on.

Index

A

Anglo-Saxon world map 25

atlases 24

axis of rotation 21

B

bathymetric maps 23

Bedolina map 25

Big Dipper 35

C

cardinal directions 14

cartographers 8, 10, 11

city maps 5, 9

climate change 28–29

climate maps 27

climate zones 6

compasses 14, 15

   experiment 40–41

contour lines 23

coordinates 16

D

degrees 16

digital maps 32

directions, compass 14–15, 35

distances 10–11

E

Earth, hemispheres 14, 17, 20–21

Eartha globe 12

Eastern Hemisphere 17

elevation 22, 23

equator 16, 17

experiments

   making a compass 40–41

   treasure map 38–39

F

floor plans 5

G

geocaching 36–37

geography 6

Global Positioning System (GPS) 32, 33, 37

globes 12–13

Google Maps 6

H

hemispheres 14, 17, 20–21

hikers 41, 42–43

   scales 10

   topographic maps 23

   trail maps 7

historical maps 5, 24–25

I

Imago Mundi map 25

international date line 19

L

latitude 16–17

legends 9

London Underground 31

longitude 16–17

   and time zones 18–19

M

map keys 8–9

maps

   defined 4–5

   deforestation 27

   why we need 6–7

modern mapping 32–33

N

navigation 15, 34–35

north arrows 15

Northern Hemisphere 14

North Pole 20, 34, 35

North Star/Polaris 14, 34–5

O

orbit, Earth's 21

P

physical maps 5, 22–3
Polaris (North Star) 14, 34–35
poles 16
   North 20, 34, 35
   South 20
population density maps 27
prime meridian 16, 17, 18

R

Ring of Fire 6
road maps 7
roses, compass 14, 15

S

satellite navigation systems
   (satnav) 33
satellites 28, 33
scales 10–11
seasons 21
sextants 34
sky maps 24
smartphones 32
solstice 20
South America, map 39
South Pole 20
stars, navigation 15, 34–35
street maps 7
symbols 8–9

T

thematic maps 26–7
time zones 18–19
topographic maps 22–23
trail maps 7
transit maps 30–31
treasure maps 4
   experiment 38–39
Turin papyrus map 25

W

waterways 7
Western Hemisphere 17

Acknowlegments

The publisher would like to thank the following for their kind permission to reproduce their photographs:

(Key: a-above; b-below/bottom; c-center; f-far; l-left; r-right; t-top)

Alamy Stock Photo: Kazuo Ogawa / Aflo 13cr, Rubens Alarcon 9cl, Sally Anderson 37cra, Backyard Productions 18cra, Tolo Balaguer 25tc, Andrew Beattie 33b, Serhii Chrucky 9cla, 11cla, Angela Cini 21br, Mykola Davydenko 14crb, dpa picture alliance / Thomas Eisenhuth 37clb, eye35.pix 9clb, funkyfood London - Paul Williams 25br, Peter Hermes Furian 16-17b, 20br, Liz Garnett 31bl, Global Warming Images / Ashley Cooper 28cra, Granger, NYC. 25cra, Kenneth Grant 9crb, 11crb, Richard Green 9cb, Soberka Richard / Hemis.fr 30cra, Valerii Honcharuk 7br, Peter Horree 9tc, Hum Images 27tl, incamerastock 41br, itakdalee 15tr, Johner Images 32b, Dimitrios Karamitros 6b, Steven J. Kazlowski 29br, O Kemppainen 23br, Ivan Kmit 12-13, Bruce Leighty 31br, LightField Studios 7bl, Old Images 24-25, le Moal Olivier 15bl, Panther Media GmbH / rclassen 32tr, Min Hee Park 5 (School icon), 9 (School icon x2), 11 (School icon x2), PaulPaladin 35bl, Photimageon 36tr, Photoco 15tl, PSL Images 12clb, ronstik 23bl, Science History Images / Jessica Wilson / NASA 28-29b, Science History Images / Photo Researchers 21t, 23tr, SiberianArt 27tr, Cigdem Simsek 33t, Spring Images 42-43, Pavel Stasevich 5br, 9 (Test tube icon x2), 11 (Test tube icon x2), Alan Dyer / Stocktrek Images 35br, Taplight 37crb, 37br, David Tefft 34, The History Collection 25cb, Stas Tolstnev 10, Tonellophotography 36-37b, Universal Images Group North America LLC / DeAgostini / D'Arco Editori 19tl, US Coast Guard Photo 34br, Michael Wheatley 37tc, YAY Media 13br; **Dreamstime.com:** Satjawat Boontanataweepol 30bc, Alexandre Paes Leme Dur o 17cra, Peter Hermes Furian 7t, Icons Home 5 (Building icon), 9 (Building icon x2), 11 (Building icon x2), Jevtic 26bl, Jktu21 18b, Valeriy Kaplun 3, 5cl, 14-15, Marco Livolsi 5 (Post office icon), 9 (Post office icon x2), 11 (Post office icon x2), Lukrecije 5tr, Jirapong Manastrong 31cla, Farrukh Maqbool 5 (Mail icon), 9 (Mail icon x2), 11 (Mail icon x2), Seamartini 30b, Narges Sultana 9 (Tree Icon x2), 11 (Tree Icon x2), Tupungato 16tr, Vladyslav Tykhonov 9 (Book icon x2), 11 (Book icon x2), Xileodesigns 9 (Dollar icon x2), 9 (River icon), 11 (Dollar icon x2), 11 (River icon); **Getty Images / iStock:** DigitalVision Vectors / pop_jop 4-5, duncan1890 39br, jack0m 13tr; **Science Photo Library:** Felix Pharand-Deschenes, Globaia / Hansen / UMD / Google / USGS / NASA 27b; **Shutterstock.com:** agsaz 8tr, Denis Belitsky 15br, CarryLove 19tr, Angela Cini 21bl, EmLion 22clb, Matthias Hartmann 5 (Hospital Icon), 9 (Hospital Icon x2), 11 (Hospital Icon x2), Dolores M. Harvey 9cra, LeonidKos 7cr, Thomas La Mela 26tr, New Africa 8b, Pandora Pictures 19bl, sadao 19br, West Texas Aerials 11tr, YueStock 35t

Cover images: *Front:* **123RF.com:** Anton Balazh / antartis bl; **Shutterstock.com:** Andrei Armiagov cr, AustralianCamera br, Triff t; *Back:* **Alamy Stock Photo:** LightField Studios cl, Old Images tl, Science History Images bl